HOW THEY MADE THINGS WORK!
THE ROMANS

Written by Richard Platt • Illustrated by David Lawrence

SEA-TO-SEA

Mankato Collingwood London

This edition first published in 2011 by
Sea-to-Sea Publications
Distributed by Black Rabbit Books
P.O. Box 3263, Mankato, Minnesota 56002

Printed in China, Dongguan

Library of Congress Cataloging-in-Publication Data

Platt, Richard.
 The Romans / written by Richard Platt ; illustrated by David Lawrence.
    p. cm. -- (How they made things work!)
 Includes index.
 ISBN 978-1-59771-290-3 (library binding)
 1. Technology--Rome--History--Juvenile literature. 2. Technological
innovations--Rome--History--Juvenile literature. 3. Rome--Civilization--
Juvenile literature.
I. Lawrence, David, 1959- II. Title.
 T16.P535 2011
 609.37--dc22

                                        2009044877

9 8 7 6 5 4 3 2

Published by arrangement with the Watts Publishing Group Ltd,
London.

Editor in Chief John C. Miles
Editor Sarah Ridley
Art Director Jonathan Hair
Designers Rachel Hamdi and Holly Fulbrook
Picture research Sarah Smithies

Picture credits:
Andrea Krause, istockphoto: 17 (c). Bettmann, Corbis: 17 (bl). Brian
Hoffman, Alamy: 26. Christophe Boisvieux, Corbis: 9. Danilo Ascione,
istockphoto: 17 (tr). Eckhard Slawik, Science Photo Library: 16. Hervé
Champollion, akg-images: 7. Jack Sullivan, Alamy: 23. Jeremy Voisey,
istockphoto: 12. Jupiter Images, Agence Images, Alamy: 15. Larry
Mulvehill, Science Photo Library: 19. Martin Child, Digital Vision, Getty
Images: 29. Peter Connolly, akg-images: 25. Visual Arts Library
(London), Alamy: 11.

March 2010
RD/6000006414/002

Contents

How the Romans Made Things Work .4

Concrete 6

The Arch 8

Books with Pages 10

Spectacle Entertainment 12

Waterwheels .14

Calendar 16

Roads 18

Water Supply 20

Mechanical Artillery 22

Sewers 24

Heating 26

The Dome 28

Glossary/Web Sites 30

Index 32

HOW THE ROMANS MADE THINGS WORK

In the middle of Italy's boot-shaped land, modern Rome is a great, exciting, bustling capital city. Two thousand years ago, Rome was all these things—and much more. For Roman people ruled most of the known world. They used technology and invention to control, expand, and strengthen their empire.

Ave!

Roads and War Machines

Warfare had made Rome strong. Roman soldiers were fierce, brave, and disciplined fighters. Military inventors gave them great advantages in winning battles. These skilled inventors created war machines, both big and small, to hurl missiles with deadly accuracy at the enemy. The Romans also planned carefully when building their roads. They built a network of paved highways that enabled Roman armies to march at great speed anywhere in the empire to stop rebellions.

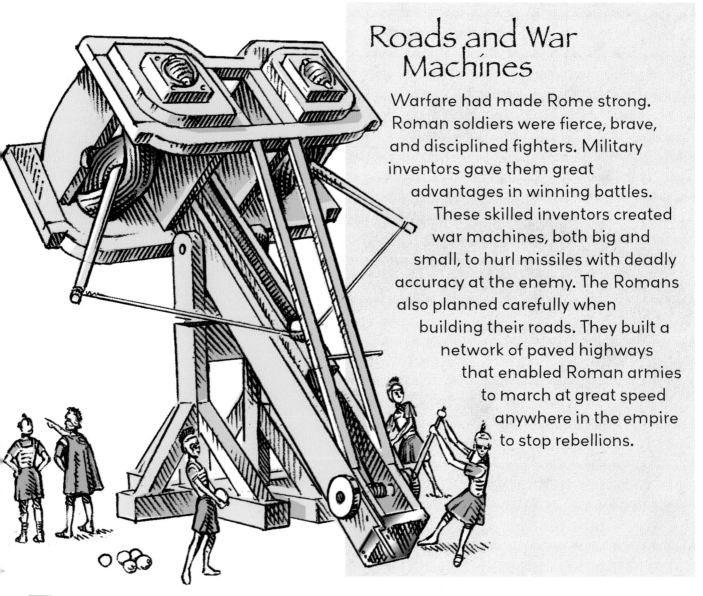

Comfortable, Healthy Cities

At home in Rome, technology had a more peaceful purpose, and was used to fill the city with grand buildings, and make the lives of the wealthy pleasant and healthy. Roman builders perfected concrete, arches, and domes. Eager to keep their city clean, the Romans piped in fresh water and built a simple sewer system. They even invented central heating to warm their public baths and later their homes.

Though few of their inventions were really new and original, Romans were experts at taking good ideas and improving them. Much of what they created still exists today—a lasting reminder of an ingenious people who valued comfort as much as conquest.

Say it in Latin!

There are phrases throughout this book in Latin, the language of the Romans. You can find out what they mean on page 31.

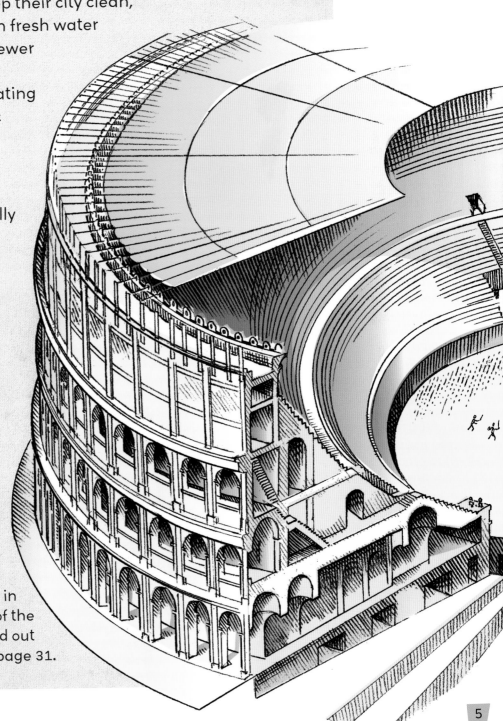

CONCRETE

Roma in una die non aedificata est.

Since ancient times, builders have glued stone blocks together with lime mortar. This powder, made by heating and crushing limestone, sets hard when mixed with water. But, in about 300 B.C., the Romans made an amazing discovery. They found that if they added the right kind of sand to the "glue," they could make walls without any stone blocks. Today, the new material they invented—concrete —is part of every building.

Baffled Builders

Rome was having a building boom, but constructing new buildings was slow and costly. Brick wasn't grand enough for government buildings, and stone such as marble had three disadvantages: it was hard to cut and carve, skilled masons were needed to work it, and it was expensive. A new material was needed urgently.

Workers mixed the special sand with "slaked lime" cement, which they stored in pottery jars until they needed it.

To make the concrete strong, they added just enough water to make a thick paste.

Stirring the concrete made sure that the sand, lime, and water mixed thoroughly.

Sandy Solution

When Roman workers making mortar mixed in sand from the town of Pozzuoli, the mixture set as hard as rock—even under water. The "sand" was actually ash from Vesuvius, a nearby volcano. It contained special chemicals that reacted with the lime.

The workers realized that they could pound the gray paste into molds to shape entire walls. Then a thin layer of marble was placed in front of the concrete to disguise its dull gray surface.

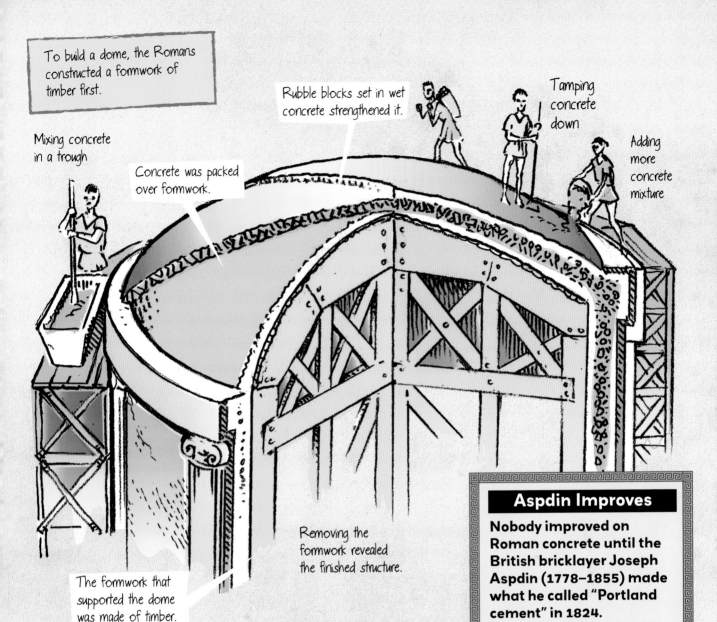

To build a dome, the Romans constructed a formwork of timber first.

Mixing concrete in a trough

Concrete was packed over formwork.

Rubble blocks set in wet concrete strengthened it.

Tamping concrete down

Adding more concrete mixture

Removing the formwork revealed the finished structure.

The formwork that supported the dome was made of timber.

Aspdin Improves

Nobody improved on Roman concrete until the British bricklayer Joseph Aspdin (1778–1855) made what he called "Portland cement" in 1824.

Trajan's Market

Molded concrete was used to make many of the arches of Trajan's Market, which was built in Rome around A.D. 110. The walls of the shops on the ground floor were once decorated with mosaic tiles.

THE ARCH

Striding boldly across a valley on thick stone legs, a Roman bridge holds a water channel nearly 160 feet (50 meters) up in the air. Built entirely without cement, this extraordinary bridge still stands, some 2,000 years after its construction. To make it possible, the Romans invented a new kind of structure: the arch.

Stupui videre te hic!

Weak Stone

Stone is strong when squeezed, but breaks easily when stretched and bent. So stone slabs used in buildings had to be massive—and very short. In a building where stone lintels (beams) held up walls and roof, the doorways, rooms, and windows were very small. Stone bridges were only used over narrow streams.

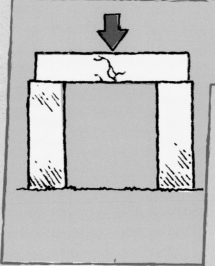

Force acts on stone lintel and cracks it.

Arch spreads load evenly so that supports take the strain.

Arch Solution

Roman builders made arches out of carefully shaped blocks. First, though, they made wooden frames called centering, to hold up the blocks during construction. Once the last block at the top, called the keystone, was in place, the arch supported itself. Then the centering could be removed.

Building an Arch

The wooden centering, shaped like a half-circle, holds up the blocks until the arch is complete.

Centering built over supporting pillars

Stones forming one-half of arch in place.

The Pont du Gard

The Pont du Gard is a bridge in southern France that carries an aqueduct (see pages 20–21). It was built to bring water to the Roman city of Nîmes. Roman architects built the Pont du Gard with three rows of arches, because the pillars supporting taller arches would have been too slim, and might have buckled and fallen. Triple arches could be made more solid.

The Pont du Gard, built by the Romans, still stands today.

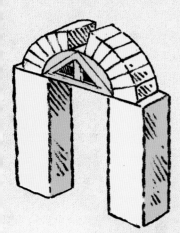

Stones forming other half of arch in place.

Keystone pushing down at top of arch keeps it in place.

Completed arch

BOOKS WITH PAGES

The book you're reading is a miracle of Roman information technology! Look closely: each sheet of paper between the covers is cleverly hinged along one edge. You can flick through easily, and move instantly from the beginning to the end. Sounds obvious? So why didn't anybody think of it before the Roman general Julius Caesar (100–44 B.C.)?

Da mihi volumen, sis?

Skip to the End of the Scroll

Before there were books as we know them, people read from scrolls (1). These were written, by hand, across long strips of paper or animal skin. Rolling the strip up made it easy to store and carry. Reading it wasn't as easy, though. To go from the beginning to the end, you had a lot of unrolling to do.

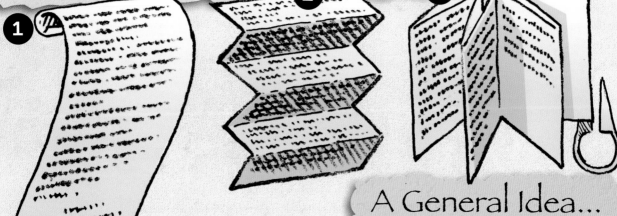

A General Idea...

According to Roman legends, when Julius Caesar was conquering France in about 50 B.C. he folded up long scrolls he received from Rome into equal-sized zigzag pages (2). Then people began to write across the zigzags (3). The idea of sewing half the folds together and cutting the others, to make what we now call a codex (4), came later.

The Codex Sinaiticus is a 1,700-year-old Bible. It was written when the Romans were still powerful.

Manuscript Marvels

Today we call a book a codex when its pages are handwritten. Proper books began with the invention of printing in the 1400s.

Before Caesar, Romans already used books of a kind—but they had only two pages. They scribbled notes on wax-covered wooden tablets hinged along one edge.

New Technology

The invention of the codex also introduced another idea we take for granted: writing in columns. Placed side-by-side, these narrow strips of words make reading easier. When you read to the bottom of one column, you start again at the top of the next one to the right.

SPECTACLE ENTERTAINMENT

Verbera eum!

A deafening roar fills the giant stadium. Fifty thousand people cheer the plucky sailors fighting a mock naval battle. Then the "ocean" drains away. Fierce jungle animals spring onto the sand, and another dramatic combat begins. It sounds just like a modern circus, but this show took place in Rome 1,900 years ago.

Bloodthirsty Romans

Rome's rulers worried about their popularity. If the Roman people didn't like them, they might overthrow them. To please the people, the emperors staged munera: fights to the death between gladiators (warrior slaves). However, nowhere in Rome was big enough to hold all the people who wanted to watch the shows.

A *myrmillo*, with his fishlike helmet (left, takes on a *retiarius* armed with a trident and net.

Massive Marvel

Roman emperor Vespasian (A.D. 9–79) ordered a vast new amphitheater (a type of stadium) and named it the Colosseum. Much of it was built of concrete (see page 6). It had 80 wide arches (see page 8). These allowed the crowds to quickly fill the stadium and leave just as fast when the show ended. The giant stadium had numbered seats and tickets, and huge, movable shades to keep the sun off the crowds. A nearby aqueduct supplied the water used to flood the arena.

Vespasian's amazing stadium still stands in the center of Rome, though the statues that once stood in 240 of its arches were removed long ago.

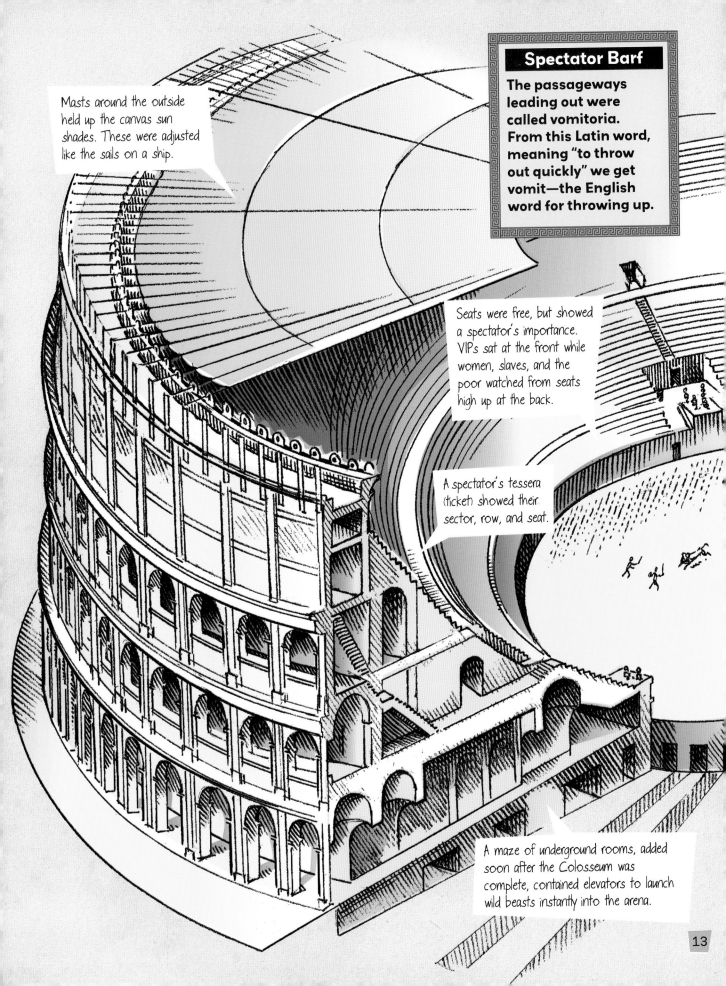

Masts around the outside held up the canvas sun shades. These were adjusted like the sails on a ship.

Spectator Barf

The passageways leading out were called vomitoria. From this Latin word, meaning "to throw out quickly" we get vomit—the English word for throwing up.

Seats were free, but showed a spectator's importance. VIPs sat at the front while women, slaves, and the poor watched from seats high up at the back.

A spectator's tessera (ticket) showed their sector, row, and seat.

A maze of underground rooms, added soon after the Colosseum was complete, contained elevators to launch wild beasts instantly into the arena.

WATERWHEELS

Grinding grain by hand is hard work. It takes two hours to mill enough flour for three loaves. This didn't matter when war and conquest provided the Romans with prisoners to work as slaves in mills. But when the empire weakened in the third century A.D., the supply of slaves dried up. Then bakers looked for a new source of power.

Medicam turbo!

Muscle Mills

The Romans knew about waterwheels, but preferred muscle-powered mills, such as the one below, when slaves were cheap. When the price of slaves rose, the Romans realized that existing millwheels did not work well. They needed a supply of fast-flowing water, and they turned too slowly, grinding enough grain for just one family.

At most bakers, pairs of slaves turned huge stones, shaped like an hourglass, to grind flour.

Current Affairs

When Germanic people attacked Rome in A.D. 537, they broke the aqueducts that supplied water to the mills. To avoid starvation, the general defending the city rebuilt the mills on barges. Moored on the Tiber River, the wheels turned in the current.

Wheely Great Idea

To make sure the water wheel would turn in slow-flowing Italian rivers, the Roman made the wheel bigger, turned the wheel on its side, and fitted more paddles. But fixed upright in the mill, the wheel could not drive grindstones directly. So an ingenious Roman used simple peg-and-cage gears to make the power "go around a corner" and turn a pair of level millstones set above.

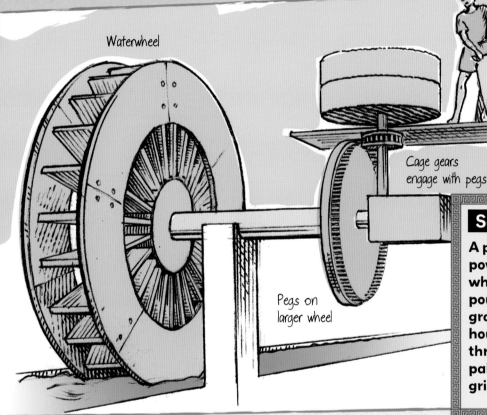

Waterwheel

Cage gears engage with pegs

Pegs on larger wheel

This improved wheel is called a "Vitruvian" water wheel, after the writer Vitruvius (ca. 80 B.C.–A.D. 25) who first described it. People across Europe copied the Roman design, and by the Middle Ages, most water mills worked like this.

Sell Those Slaves!

A pair of grindstones powered by a water wheel could turn 33–44 pounds (15–20 kg) of grain into flour every hour. This was twice or three times what a pair of slaves could grind with a hand mill.

French Flour

None of the Roman waterwheels have survived, but at Barbegal, in France, you can still see the remains of a giant mill they powered (left). The 16 pairs of grindstones that turned here milled nearly 33 tons of flour a day, enough to make bread for 80,000 people. An aqueduct brought water to power the wheels.

CALENDAR

Da mihi vinum.

Romans called it the "Year of Confusion." Julius Caesar had changed the calendar so it matched the passing seasons. But to fix the problem, and to make sure that every following year was just the right length, 46 B.C. had to have an extra 11 weeks. The year lasted a whopping 445 days.

Mixed-up Months

Romans measured their months using the moon's phases. There are 28 days between each full moon, making a Roman year 12 x 28 = 336 days. Romans thought that 366 ¼ days passed between one midsummer day and the next. So to make the calendar match the seasons they added an extra month every eight years. Unfortunately, they were wrong! Every year, the calendar and the seasons drifted one more day apart.

Earth goes around the Sun once every 365 ¼ days.

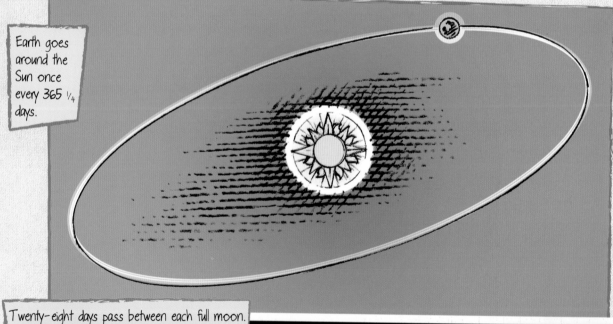

Twenty-eight days pass between each full moon.

Caesar's Calendar

Julius Caesar asked the best astronomers to fix the problem. The Greek-Egyptian expert Sosigenes told Caesar that each year actually lasted 365 1/4 days. He suggested a calendar 365 days long, adding an extra day every four years. The calendar, named "Julian" after Julius Caesar, worked so well that (with a little adjusting 15 centuries later), it has been in use ever since.

Julius Caesar gave his name to the calendar used for centuries.

When Caesar reformed the calendar, harvest time was two months out of step with the seasons.

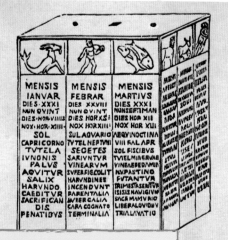

This Roman calendar is in the form of a stone block. It has the signs of the zodiac carved into it.

Not Quite Right

Caesar's changes weren't quite right. Each year actually lasts not 365 days and 6 hours, but 365 days, 5 hours, 49 minutes and 15.974 seconds. So the Julian calendar drifted a day each 128 years. To fix this, Pope Gregory XIII changed the calendar again in 1582. His Gregorian calendar skips a leap year each century—unless the year can be divided by 400. This calendar still isn't quite perfect, but will only be one day wrong by the year 3500.

ROADS

Viaene omnes vere Romam ducunt?

Stretching away into the distance, a wide road carves a straight line across a European landscape. Far beneath the black, shiny asphalt lies an ancient track of crushed stone and gravel. This route is more than 2,000 years old. The Romans built it to enable their armies to march to the farthest points of their spreading empire.

Rotten Roads

Horses' hooves and cartwheels quickly turned roads to dust in the summer. Winter rains made them into sticky swamps that swallowed vehicles. Fast, efficient land transportation was essential for trade—and later for conquest. So the Romans had to find a way to build better roads.

Solid Base

Flooding quickly made roads collapse, so Roman roadbuilders first dug trenches on either side to drain the route. Then they dug out the base of the road, replacing mud with layers of sand, stone, and concrete. A top layer of cobblestones finished the road. Built like this, Roman roads could withstand even the heaviest carts.

A Roman surveyor uses a groma to get the road straight.

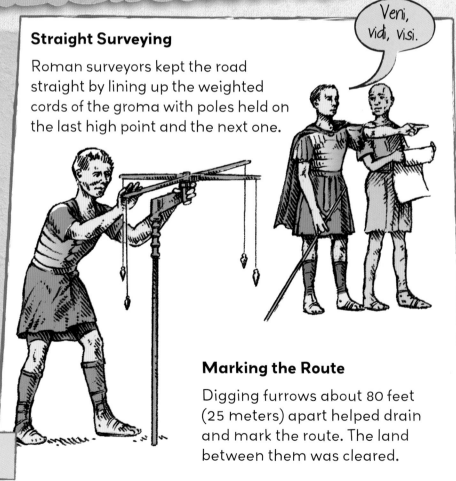

Straight Surveying

Roman surveyors kept the road straight by lining up the weighted cords of the groma with poles held on the last high point and the next one.

Veni, vidi, visi.

Marking the Route

Digging furrows about 80 feet (25 meters) apart helped drain and mark the route. The land between them was cleared.

Tiberian Triumph

Roman roads made very fast journeys possible. Tiberius (who later became emperor) set a record when he raced to see his dying brother in 9 B.C. He covered 200 miles (320 km) in a day, wearing out three chariots on the way. Nobody traveled farther in one day until railroad tracks crossed Europe in the 1800s.

A section of Roman road still in existence. Many Roman roads form the basis of the major European highways today.

Firm Foundations

Soldiers building the road dug a trench 40 inches (1 meter) deep and 10–22 feet (3–7 meters) wide, with drainage ditches on either side.

Building Up the Road

A variety of building materials were laid down next, including sand, mortar, blocks and slabs, concrete and crushed stone, and, to finish off, a final top layer of stones.

Edging the road with heavy curb stones stopped it from spreading in use.

Top layer of tight-fitting stones, gently curved to throw off rain

Concrete with crushed stone

Blocks and slabs in mortar

Trench

Mortar

Sand

19

WATER SUPPLY

Rome was a city of water. It sprayed from fountains. It splashed without stopping from free public faucets in the street. For the price of the smallest coin, Romans could soak in steaming hot water at the public baths. Today this hardly seems surprising. But 20 centuries ago bringing water to Rome was an amazing achievement.

Water Woes

Rome's population was huge, and growing. It was the biggest city in the ancient world and, in A.D. 50, one million people lived there. Some of the water they needed for drinking and washing came from local wells. But they needed much, much more water than that. But between Rome and the water the Romans needed, stood hills and valleys.

Water level had to drop 40 inches each mile (1 meter every 2 kilometers) to keep it flowing.

To bridge small low points, the Romans placed the aqueduct up on a wall.

To cross lower valleys, they built an arcade (a bridge with arches).

Where possible, the aqueduct snaked around hills, so that the water went very gently downhill.

Tunnels cut through a few hilltops.

Roman surveyors used instruments like this chorobates to plan the route of aqueducts. When the plumblines (weighted cords) crossed the lines marked on the frame, the bench on top was exactly level. Looking along it allowed surveyors to see how much higher or lower the land ahead was.

Cross-Country

To bring more water to their city, the Romans built channels, called aqueducts. To make the water flow, the aqueducts had to slope downward at a precise angle. To keep this gentle slope constant, they used accurate measuring tools, and made the channels snake around the landscape. They built high bridges to cross valleys, and tunnels to go through hills.

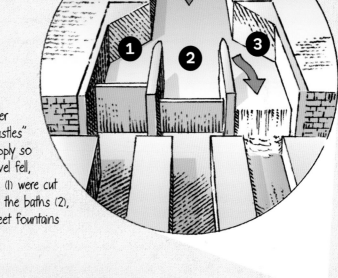

Aqua Facts

To carry water across a valley near Lyon, in France, the Romans made pipes from 11,000 tons of lead.

The water that fills Rome's famous Trevi Fountain still comes from the Aqua Virgo, a Roman aqueduct built more than 2,000 years ago.

In towns, water towers or "castles" divided the supply so that as the level fell, private homes (1) were cut off first, then the baths (2), and public street fountains (3) last of all.

Settling tanks removed dirt and pebbles.

They took water across the deepest gorges using pressurized pipes.

Awash

In A.D. 100, everyone in Rome had as much water as each person in NYC had in 1900.

MECHANICAL ARTILLERY

Fighting a Roman army was a frightening experience. As well as the arrows and spears that all soldiers threw, the Romans used terrifying war machines. Powered by twisted animal gristle, they hurled arrows as big as broomsticks, and stone balls the weight of refrigerators. These mighty catapults could hit targets up to 2,130 feet (650 meters) away, and were more accurate than any archer.

Where's the Target?

Earlier war machines, developed in Greece, had two major problems. Their wooden frames were so bulky they hid the target from view, making aiming difficult. In addition, the bundles of animal gristle that powered them stretched when they got wet, so they were useless when it rained.

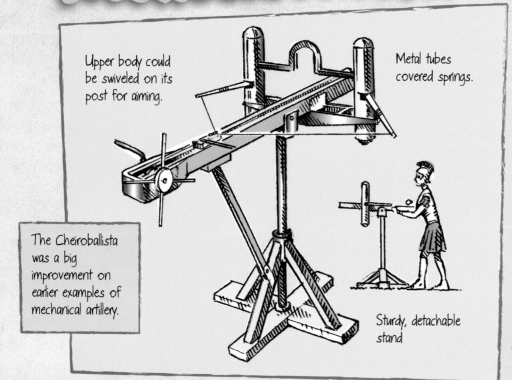

Upper body could be swiveled on its post for aiming.

Metal tubes covered springs.

The Cheiroballista was a big improvement on earlier examples of mechanical artillery.

Sturdy, detachable stand

Smaller, Lighter

The Romans replaced the wooden frames of smaller catapults with much slimmer metal parts. This created an open frame that warriors could aim just like a modern rifle. Copper or bronze tubes covering the gristle springs made the catapults into all-weather weapons.

Superheroes

The Romans considered the inventors who designed spring-powered missile throwers to be heroes. They were the rock stars of the ancient world.

Really big siege engines like the ballista were designed to smash down city walls with stones.

Actors load a modern reproduction of a small Roman ballista-type weapon.

The Ballista

This huge Roman siege engine also utilized twisted-sinew springs. Winching back the arms built up massive tension in order to power stone projectiles through the air.

Twisted sinew springs

Winch for pulling back rope

Shaped stones of equal weight

SEWERS

We live in a "flush-and-forget" age, but the Romans were not so lucky. So many poor Romans emptied pots full of sewage from their windows that the city government passed a law to punish those who soaked passersby. Wealthy Romans who could afford it had lavatories (toilets) linked to an efficient sewer system.

Fue! Odor horribilis!

Stinking Streets

As Rome grew, it began to stink. Most Romans used pottery jars as lavatories. A smelly cart arrived at night to remove the contents, which were tipped on fields to make crops grow. But a lot of sewage still ended up on the streets, causing a odor problem and attracting flies that spread disease.

Dynamic Drain

The Romans had built a huge gully, the Cloaca Maxima, in the seventh century B.C., to drain marshland so they could build the city's forum (marketplace). A network of sewer pipes carried rainwater into the Cloaca Maxima from city streets. Street sweepers washed street waste into the sewers. Eventually, the sewers also drained public lavatories and some private homes.

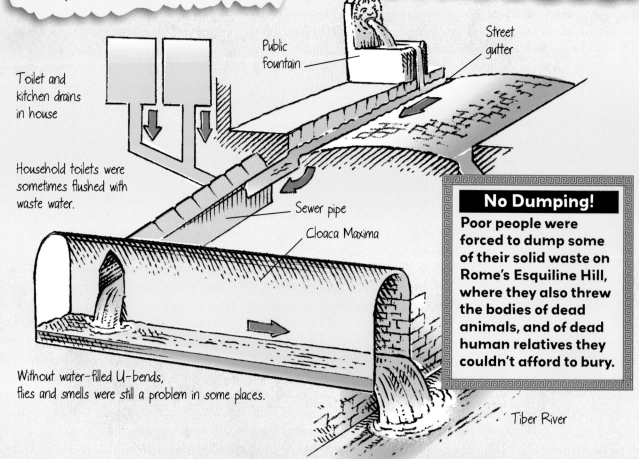

Toilet and kitchen drains in house

Public fountain

Street gutter

Household toilets were sometimes flushed with waste water.

Sewer pipe

Cloaca Maxima

Without water-filled U-bends, flies and smells were still a problem in some places.

Tiber River

No Dumping!
Poor people were forced to dump some of their solid waste on Rome's Esquiline Hill, where they also threw the bodies of dead animals, and of dead human relatives they couldn't afford to bury.

Da mihi spongiam, sis.

Roman public washrooms were friendly places. Men and women sat side-by-side on marble seats. Instead of toilet paper, there were sponges on sticks, kept clean in a trough of water that ran around the floor.

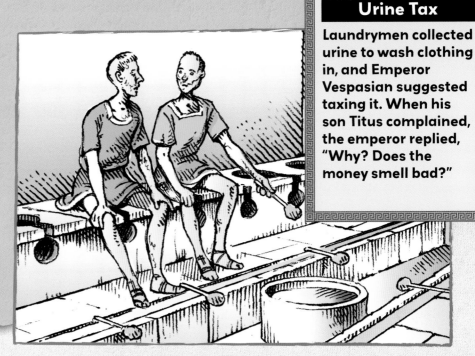

The Cloaca Maxima was 16 feet (5 meters) in diameter. It was beautifully constructed of fitted stone blocks. All the main sewers were big enough to row boats through for inspection.

Look Out!

This is a blank-verse translation of a poem by the poet Juvenal (late first–early second century A.D.), describing the hazards of going out and about in the streets in Rome:

Think of the number of times cracked or broken pots fall out of the windows, of the amount of weight they bring down with a crash onto the street and dent the sidewalk. Anyone who goes out for dinner without making a will is a fool...you can suffer as many deaths as there are open windows to pass under. So send up a prayer that people will be content with just emptying out their slop bowls!

HEATING

Even sunny Rome had gray winter days. If the weather got REALLY cold, Romans flocked to the baths. There, the fire heating the water also warmed the walls and floor. When Romans invaded northern countries, the colder climate made them shiver and feel homesick. So they built their homes like their favorite baths in Rome, with underfloor heating called hypocausts.

Nonne aura calida in togam est bona!

That Frosty Feeling

Rome gets very hot in summer, so Roman homes were built to be cool. In the winter, those who could afford to heated their homes with charcoal stoves, called braziers. They were a lot like today's barbecues. But braziers did not provide enough heat to keep out the chilly frosts in the northern parts of the Roman Empire.

Surprising Fact!

Roman baths heated by hypocausts were noisy places. The Roman writer Seneca lived above one, and complained of the screams when slaves plucked the hairs of their master's armpits.

Winter Warmer

A furnace outside the house supplied hot air for the hypocaust. To allow the hot air to circulate beneath the floor, Roman builders supported it on short columns. Tiles covered the gaps between them. After swirling beneath the floor, the hot air rose through flues (chimneys) running through the walls, and these got hot, too.

This surviving Roman hypocaust clearly shows the bases of the pillars that supported the tiled floor above.

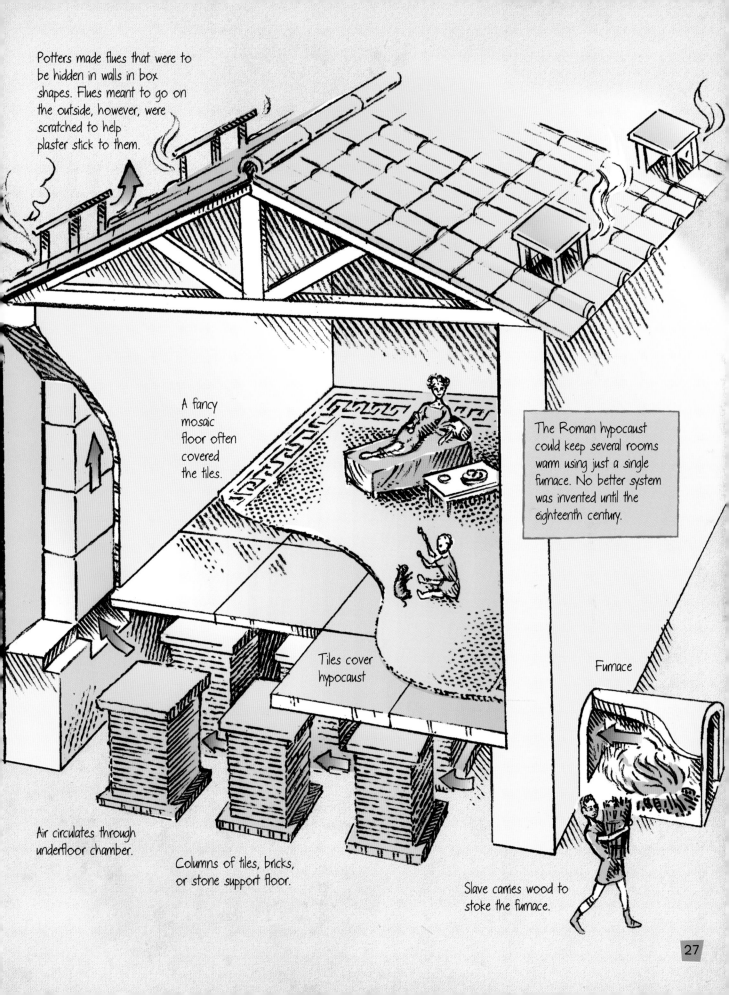

Potters made flues that were to be hidden in walls in box shapes. Flues meant to go on the outside, however, were scratched to help plaster stick to them.

A fancy mosaic floor often covered the tiles.

The Roman hypocaust could keep several rooms warm using just a single furnace. No better system was invented until the eighteenth century.

Tiles cover hypocaust

Furnace

Air circulates through underfloor chamber.

Columns of tiles, bricks, or stone support floor.

Slave carries wood to stoke the furnace.

THE DOME

As Roman architects made bigger and grander buildings, they ran into the problem of how to hold the roof up. Adding extra supports was an easy answer. However, in really enormous buildings, the rooms were soon so crowded with columns that you couldn't see to the other side. A better solution was to build an arch that spread out in every direction.

Roof Woes

The bigger a building is, the bigger and heavier its roof needs to be. Roman builders knew that roofs made of timber could be light, and span wide, open rooms. But timber roofs were not fireproof. Lintels (stone beams) created fireproof roofs, but in wide rooms they needed to be held up by supporting columns.

Concrete to the Rescue

The answer was to combine two brilliant ideas: concrete (page 6) and arches (page 8).
Arches could span great distances, as long as they had strong foundations to stop the top from pushing the sides apart. Concrete had great strength, and it could be made light in weight by stirring in foamy, air-filled pumice rock.

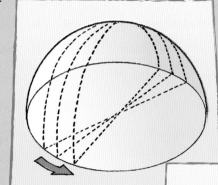

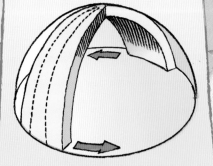

By rotating the apex, or top, of an arch (above) and creating a solid structure from that shape, the clever Romans came up with another excellent idea, which was the dome (right).

Amazing Pantheon

The greatest achievement of the Roman dome-builders was the Pantheon, a vast temple built in A.D. 125 to honor the many Roman gods. Its huge dome was built so solidly that it still stands today. No other building had a circular dome this big until the invention of steel-strengthened concrete more than 1,700 years later.

Dome weighs approximately 4,960 tons.

Instead of a keystone, the dome has an extremely strong ring of bronze.

Central oculus (eye) provides light and ventilation, and reduces weight. It is more than 27 feet (8 meters) wide.

Serve You Right!

Three tennis courts would fit neatly inside the Pantheon dome, though balls might bounce off the concrete walls.

Bubbly pumice stone keeps concrete light at the top.

To reduce weight, dome is much thinner (4 feet (1.2 meters)) at the top than it is at the bottom (21 feet (6.4 meters)).

Sunken panels make the dome lighter. They originally had stars painted in them.

Fist-size lumps of extra-hard rock were mixed in to strengthen the thick concrete at the base.

Unsafe!

No one would be allowed to build the Pantheon today. Because the structure contains no steel bars for added strength, modern building inspectors would consider it dangerously unsafe.

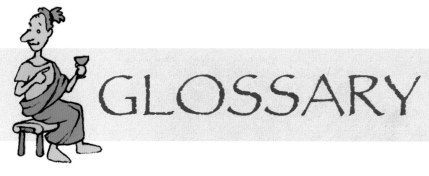

GLOSSARY

aim To point a weapon at a TARGET.

amphitheater Circular or egg-shaped stadium.

arch Curving brick or stone support for a wall or roof, making an opening below.

artillery War engine for hurling weapons.

astronomer Scientist who studies the stars.

cartwheel Hard wooden wheel turning on a cart.

catapult Weapon, powered by a spring, usually used to hurl stones.

cement Powder used to make MORTAR.

centering Temporary frame that supports an ARCH during construction.

chorobates SURVEYING instrument used to pick out points of equal height.

cobblestone Large rounded stone once used for road surfaces.

codex Handwritten book.

curbstone Heavy stone placed at the edge of a road to stop the surface from spreading.

current A flow, such as the rush of water in a river.

dome Roof shaped like an upside-down bowl.

flue A chimney or hot-air pipe in a wall.

formwork MOLD for concrete used to make a building or part of it.

forum Roman market- and meeting-place.

furrow Deep groove cut in the ground.

gladiator SLAVE trained to fight in combats staged in the AMPHITHEATER.

grind To crush into a powder.

grindstones A pair of rough round stones, one of which turns, MILLING anything placed between them.

gristle Tough, springy fiber that holds together the bones of an animal.

groma SURVEYING instrument made with four PLUMBLINES hanging from a pair of crossed sticks.

gully Large underground pipe.

hourglass A glass bottle with a narrow waist, used like a clock: sand inside takes 60 minutes to trickle through from the top half to the bottom half.

hypocaust Roman hot-air underfloor heating system.

keystone Central top block in an ARCH.

laundryman A man who washes clothes and cloth.

lead Soft, gray metal that is easy to shape.

leap year Every fourth year, having 366 days: other years have 365 days.

lime Powder used in MORTAR that sets into a hard lump when combined with water. Lime is made by heating and crushing LIMESTONE.

limestone Kind of rock used to make LIME.

lintel Strong, straight beam of timber or stone used to support the weight of a wall above a door or window.

mill To GRIND; or a building where grinding takes place.

mold Container shaped to enclose a hardening paste, such as concrete, so that when it sets the paste takes on the shape of the mold, which is then removed.

moon phase The shape of that part of the moon lit by the sun, which changes from a circle to a crescent and back each 28 days.

mortar Gluelike paste used to stick together stone or bricks to make walls or roads.

mosaic Pattern on a floor or wall made from tiny, bright-colored tiles.

munera GLADIATOR battle paid for by a wealthy Roman.

oculus Circular hole in a building, such as at the top of some DOMES.

plumber Worker who shapes lead or joins or makes water pipes.

plumbline String with a weight on one end to keep it hanging straight down.

potter Worker who shapes and bakes clay into pots.

pumice Light frothy kind of stone spewed out by a VOLCANO.

rifle A handheld gun with a long barrel (firing tube).

rubble Broken lumps of rock.

scroll Roll of writing material such as paper.

settle Falling of solid material, such as stones or sand, to the bottom of a pool of still liquid.

sewage Liquid and solid waste from the human gut and bladder.

sewer A GULLY to carry SEWAGE.

slave A captive worker, kept as the property of a free person.

steel Strong metal made mostly of iron.

survey To measure land.

tablet Small, thin, flat piece of hard material.

tamp To ram down hard.

target Something at which a weapon is fired.

temple Place of worship.

tessera Ticket.

VIP Short for very important person.

volcano Hole in the Earth's solid crust through which melted rock escapes.

COOL STUFF TO SAY IN LATIN

Page 4
Ave!
Hail! (Hello!)

Page 6
Roma in una die non aedificata est.
Rome wasn't built in a day.

Page 8
Stupui videre te hic!
Imagine seeing you here!

Page 10
Da mihi volumem, sis?
Please pass the scroll?

Page 12
Verbera eum!
Thrash him!

Page 14
Medicam turbo!
Spin doctor.

Page 16
Da mihi vinum.
Pass the wine.

Page 18
Viaene omnes vere Romam ducunt?
Do all roads lead to Rome?

Veni, vidi, visi.
I came, I saw, I inspected.

Page 24-25
Fue! Odor horribilis!
Phooey! What a stink!

Da mihi spongiam, sis.
Please pass the sponge on a stick.

Page 26
Nonne aura calida in togam est bona!
That hot air up your toga sure feels good!

WEB SITES

Construct a Roman aqueduct
http://www.pbs.org/wgbh/
nova/lostempires/roman/
aqueduct.html

Roman baths
http://www.pbs.org/wgbh/nova/
lostempires/roman/builds.html

Ancient Roman Time Line
http://www.exovedate.com/
ancient_timeline_one.html

Amphitheater
http://www.pbs.org/wnet/
warriorchallenge/gladiators/
interactive_flash.html

Note to parents and teachers:
Every effort has been made by the Publishers to ensure that the web sites in this book are suitable for children, that they are of the highest educational value, and that they contain no inappropriate or offensive material. However, because of the nature of the Internet, it is impossible to guarantee that the contents of these sites will not be altered. We strongly advise that Internet access is supervised by a responsible adult.

INDEX

amphitheater 12, 30
aqueducts 9, 12, 14, 15, 20–21
arches 5, 7, 8–9, 12, 28, 30
architects 9, 28
army 4, 18, 22–23
artillery 22–23, 30
Aspdin, Joseph 7
astronomers 17, 30

ballista 23
baths, public 5, 20, 21, 26
books 10–11, 30
bridges 8, 9, 21

Caesar, Julius 10, 11, 16, 17
calendar, Julian 16–17
catapult 22, 30
centering 8, 9, 30
Cheiroballista 22
Cloaca Maxima 24, 25
codex 10, 11, 30
Colosseum 12–13
concrete 5, 6–7, 12, 19, 28, 29, 30

domes 5, 7, 28–29, 30

empire, the 4, 14, 18, 26

flour 14–15

formwork 7, 30
fountains 20, 21
France 9, 10, 15, 21

gladiators 12, 30
grindstones 15, 30
groma 18, 30

heating, central 5
    underfloor 26–27, 30
houses 5, 21, 26–27
hypocausts 26–27, 30

Juvenal 25

lavatories 24, 25

machines, war 4, 22–23
mills 14–15, 30
mortar 6, 7, 19, 30
mosaics 7, 27, 30

Pantheon 29
Pont du Gard 8–9

roads 4, 18–19, 30
Rome 4, 5, 6, 7, 10, 12, 14, 20, 21, 24, 25, 26
roofs 28–29, 30

scrolls 10, 11, 31
sewers 5, 24–25, 31
slaves 12, 14, 15, 26, 27, 30, 31
soldiers 4, 19, 22
Sosigenes 17
stadium 12–13, 30
surveyors 18, 20

Tiberius 19
Trajan's Market 7

Vespasian, Emperor 12, 25
Vesuvius 6
Vitruvius 15

warfare 4, 8, 9, 22–23
water (supply) 5, 20–21
waterwheels 14–15